AVIATION

TBF/TBM Avenger

Grumman's First Torpedo Bomber in World War II

DAVID DOYLE

Library of Congress Control Number: 2019947425

Designed by Justin Watkinson
Technical Layout by Jack Chappell
Type set in Impact/Minion Pro/Univers LT Std
Front cover photo courtesy of Rick Kolasa

ISBN: 978-0-7643-5939-2
Printed in China

Published by Schiffer Publishing, Ltd.
4880 Lower Valley Road
Atglen, PA 19310
Phone: (610) 593-1777; Fax: (610) 593-2002
E-mail: Info@schifferbooks.com
www.schifferbooks.com

Acknowledgments

Creating this book has been very much a team effort and could not have been done without a great deal of help from many of my friends. Among those contributing to this effort are Tom Kailbourn, Rich Kolasa, Scott Taylor, Stan Piet, Dana Bell, Sean Hart, Tracy White, the staffs of the National Museum of Naval Aviation and the Naval Historical Center, Leo Polaski, the National Archives and Records Administration, and the Tailhook Association. Photos not otherwise credited were taken by the author. Through all of this, the Lord has blessed me with a wonderful and supportive wife, without whose encouragement (and scanning!), none of this would be possible. Thank you, Denise!

Contents

Introduction

When the Navy considered various proposals for a potential replacement for the TBD, the viable candidates were Grumman's XTBF and this aircraft, the Vought XTBU. *National Museum of Naval Aviation*

Even before the US was drawn into World War II by the attack on Pearl Harbor, the US Navy had recognized that their mainstay torpedo bomber, the circa 1934 Douglas Devastator, was obsolete. In 1939, the Navy had issued a requirement for a new torpedo bomber, which was to have a top speed of 300 miles per hour, be capable of carrying one 2,000-pound torpedo or three 500-pound bombs internally, feature self-sealing fuel tanks, and have a three-man crew, one of which would man the power-operated dorsal turret.

This solicitation brought proposals from a number of firms, two of which the Navy felt warranted prototypes. They were from Vought, for their XTBU-1 Sea Wolf, which would later see production as the Consolidated TBY, and from Grumman, for the XTBF-1, the subject of this book.

The XTBF-1 was Grumman's first torpedo bomber and drew heavily on the firm's experience with other naval aircraft, including notably the F4F Wildcat. The TBF-1 was substantially larger than the F4F but remained a midwing monoplane. The big torpedo bomber was to be powered by a 1,700-horsepower R-2600-8 air-cooled Wright radial engine and was armed with a dorsal .50-caliber machine gun plus a pair of .30-caliber machine guns, one in the cowling and a second in a rear-firing ventral position. Grumman engineer William T. Schwendler was largely responsible for the TBF design.

In April 1940, the Navy ordered two prototypes from Grumman and one from Vought. In December 1940, even before the first prototype had flown, the Navy ordered 286 production TBF aircraft. The first prototype flow on August 7, 1941, with Robert Leicester (Bob) Hall, Grumman's engineering test pilot, at the controls; contrary to urban myth about the origin of the name, in October 1941 the Navy designated the aircraft "Avenger." Somewhat ironically, the new torpedo bomber made its public debut at Bethpage, New York, on the afternoon of December 7, 1941.

In 1941, the US Navy's frontline torpedo bomber was the Douglas TBD Devastator. The design was showing its age and had several deficiencies. The Navy had begun seeking a replacement in 1939 and by 1940 had narrowed the field to two aircraft, the XTBF and the XTBU. *National Museum of Naval Aviation*

CHAPTER 1
XTBF-1

As was the custom for decades in the aviation industry, as the design was being finalized, a full-size mockup of the TBF was created by Grumman. Made principally of plywood, the mockup allowed the details to be honed, as fit, clearance, visibility, and ergonomics all were checked in a real-world setting. Design modifications as called for by evaluation of the mockup by Grumman engineers and representatives of the Navy could be worked out, tried, and evaluated.

Considerable effort was expended developing a workable, power-operated turret for the rear gunner. With other aircraft manufacturers having been stymied seeking similar turrets for naval aircraft from outside manufacturers, a Grumman team lead by Oscar Olsen resorted to designing their own. The result was a Plexiglas-enclosed, electrically operated turret housing the gunner and an M2 Browning .50-caliber machine gun.

Once satisfied with the design as presented by the mockup, the flyable prototype was built. That aircraft took to the air for the first time on August 7, 1941, with Bob Hall at the controls. The initial flight was followed by a series of routine test flights, which ended when the first XTBF-1 was destroyed in a crash on November 28. During a routine test flight, with Hobart Cook at the controls and engineer Gordon Israel in the back, a rapidly growing fire was found in the bomb bay. Both men safely bailed out, and the XTBF-1 plummeted into the woods near Brentwood, New York.

Fortunately, this led to only minor setbacks in the Avenger program, and the second prototype took to the air on December 20, 1941.

In April 1940, the US Navy ordered from Grumman two prototypes of the XTBF-1, which was intended to replace the Douglas TBD-1 Devastator. In advance of the prototypes, Grumman constructed this wooden mockup, shown here in September 1940 alongside a Grumman F4F Wildcat fuselage. Both aircraft had a barrel-shaped fuselage that was a characteristic of several Grumman designs in the late 1930s and early 1940s. *Leo Polaski collection*

The Grumman XTBF-1 mockup lacked the right outer wing. The outer wings on the actual prototypes were designed to fold back, so the plane would take up less valuable space on an aircraft carrier. Near the outboard end of the left wing, behind the leading edge, is a "mailbox" slot, which channeled the airflow around the wingtip so as to prevent stalling. *Leo Polaski collection*

The mockup is observed from the upper rear, showing the design of the wing, the horizontal stabilizer, the elevator, and the trim tabs on the elevator and the aileron. The frame of the canopy was sketched in with shaped rods. There were to be two cockpits, with a powered turret to the rear: a significant departure from previous Navy carrier-based bombers, with their open rear machine gun stations. A machine gun, ammo chute, and gunner's seat are installed in the representation of the turret. *National Archives*

As designed on the mockup of the XTBF-1, the aft part of the fuselage was of a conical shape, with the vertical fin and rudder positioned above it. Below and aft of the turret on the fuselage were a door with a round window, to the front of which were two more round windows. On the belly of the fuselage to the front of the tail landing gear was a manually operated Browning .30-caliber machine gun. The object mounted atop the fuselage to the front of the windscreen represented a gun camera. *Leo Polaski collection*

The XTBF-1 mockup is seen from the front left with the left wing extended. Although the propeller was made of wood, the radial engine was real, presumably a Wright R-2600. The left exhaust is painted in black on the fuselage. The XTBF-1 and subsequent models of the Avenger were to have an internal bay, with folding doors, for a torpedo or bombs, and those doors were represented on the mockup.

The XTBF-1 mockup's left wing was designed to fold back on two axes: the wings rotated so that the leading edge pointed downward, while at the same time swinging to the rear somewhat parallel to the fore-and-aft axis of the fuselage. This feature would carry over to production Avengers. *National Archives*

As seen inside the mockup, the XTBF-1 was to have a radio operator and bombardier's compartment below and aft of the turret. In the lower rear of the compartment was a flexible .30-caliber machine gun, for defense against enemy aircraft approaching from the lower aft quarter. This Browning .30-caliber machine gun is equipped with a telescopic sight surrounded by a small armor plate and an ammunition box on the left side of the receiver. To the right is a seat and seatbelt, and to the upper left is the side entry door. *Leo Polaski collection*

A Grumman employee is demonstrating the range of movement of the machine gun in the turret. This was in keeping with the purpose of a mockup: to test the fit and action of the various parts of an aircraft before committing to construction. To the right, below the canopy, is a representation of a container for a life raft. *Leo Polaski collection*

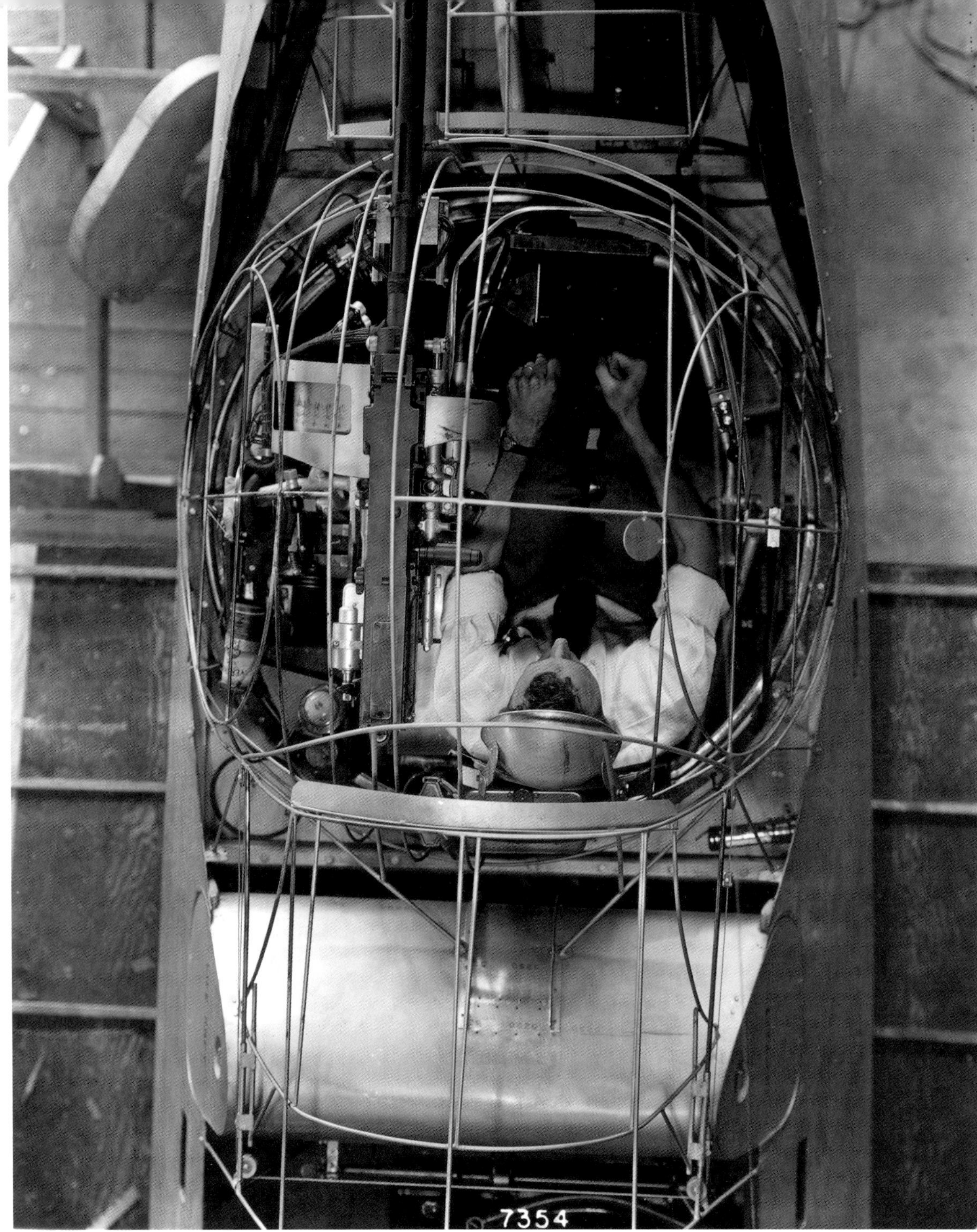

The turret of the mockup of the XTBF-1 is viewed from above with a man in the gunner's seat. As with production Avengers, the .50-caliber machine gun was offset to the left of center, and the gunner sat to the right of center. Toward the bottom of the photo is the storage container for a life raft. *Leo Polaski collection*

The cockpit of the XTBF-1 mockup was a good representation of what the actual cockpit of the XTBF-1 prototypes would look like. At the top was a telescopic gunsight. The instrument panel had placards representing the various gauges and instruments. On the XTBF-1 prototypes, the pistons alongside the rudder pedals would be on the outboard sides of the pedals. *Leo Polaski collection*

This XTBF-1 reportedly was the second of two prototypes of that model, Bureau Number (BuNo) 2540. The plane lacks the fillet that was added to the upper rear of the fuselage after it was completed. The second prototype's first flight was on December 7, 1941, the day of the Japanese attack on Pearl Harbor. Note the open bifolding-canopy sections over the rear cockpit. *Leo Polaski collection*

The second XTBF-1 prototype is viewed from the front right. The Curtiss Electric propeller blades were equipped with cuffs. The aircraft was painted in a camouflage of Nonspecular (NS) Blue Gray over NS Light Gray. Whereas the XTBF-1 mockup had a straight pitot tube at the center of the leading edge of the left wing, the pitot tube on the prototype XTBF-1s was on an outward-tilted mast near the left wingtip. *National Archives*

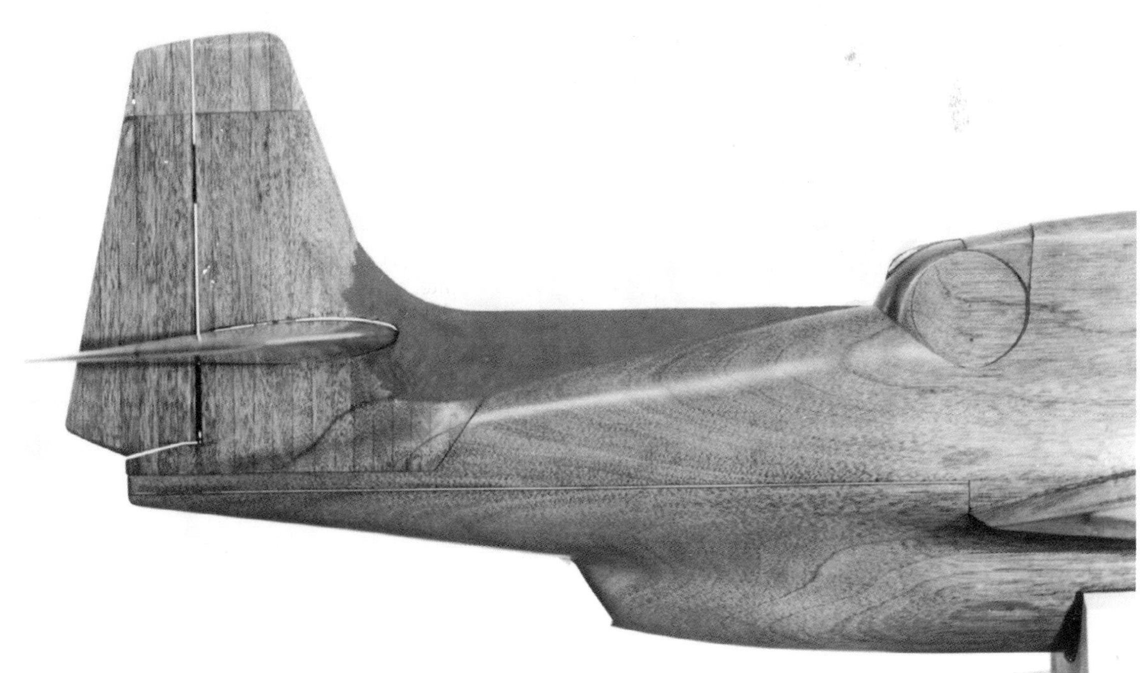

After the second XTBF-1 was completed, designers developed a fix for directional-stability problems experienced by both prototypes. This involved installing a fillet with a sharp upper edge on the fuselage to the rear of the turret, joining to the front of the dorsal fin. A proposed fillet is shown on a wooden model of the XTBF-1. *Leo Polaski collection*

The fillet, as approved, is shown installed on the second prototype XTBF-1. Unlike the model depicted in the preceding photo, the actual fillet did not extend all the way to the turret, and the junction of the top of the fillet and the leading edge of the dorsal fin was angular, not curved. *National Archives*

The wings are folded on the second prototype XTBF-1. The wings were folded, unfolded, and locked hydraulically. The center section of the wing contained three fuel tanks. Visible on the top of the cowl is a trough for a single, fixed .30-caliber machine gun that was aimed and fired by the pilot. *National Archives*

The shapes and the layout of the three small windows on the left side of the radio operator and bombardier's compartment of the second XTBF-1 prototype are seen from the left rear. These included a small, rectangular window below the wing root; a round one in the center; and an oblong one to the rear. This arrangement of windows would continue through early-production TBF-1s. Note the outward tilt of the pitot tube mast. *National Archives*

As seen on the left side of the second XTBF-1 prototype, a single exhaust stack on each side would remain a constant throughout TBF/TBM production. The radio antenna would remain in the position seen here, and at a rearward tilt, until the TBF-1C. *National Archives*

Partially hidden by the upper blade of the Curtiss Electric propeller in this frontal view of the second XTBF-1 prototype is the carburetor-air intake scoop. The slightly cranked shape of the oleo struts of the main landing gear also are evident. *National Archives*

With wheels chocked, the second prototype Grumman XTBF-1 is seen from the front with the wings folded. Note the lightening holes of varying sizes on the ribs of the outer wings. *National Archives*

From May 1942 to June 1943, the second XTBF-1 prototype was assigned to the National Advisory Committee for Aeronautics (NACA) for testing at its Langley Memorial Aeronautical Laboratory, Langley Field, Virginia. In this photo of the plane at Langley on February 24, 1943, note the air data boom, sometimes called a test probe, on the right wingtip. *NASA*

The torpedo/bomb bay of the second XTBF-1 prototype is viewed from the front with the doors open and a torpedo, likely a Mk. 13, mounted in it. On each side of the bay are three racks for transporting bombs. The dark, rectangular shape on the bulkhead at the rear of the bay was the bomb-aiming window. *Leo Polaski collection*

CHAPTER 2

TBF-1/TBM-1

As seen from the right side, the second XTBF-1 prototype could be mistaken for the early-production TBF-1, with the principal exception of the Curtiss Electric propeller with cuffed blades. *Leo Polaski collection*

Fortunately, those initial tests indicated that the Avenger was viable. Fortuitously for a nation suddenly thrust into a war, the first of the 286 production Avengers the Navy had ordered the year before, on December 23, 1940, rolled off the assembly line on January 3, 1942.

With the US now at war on two fronts, and with American forces in the Pacific losing considerable territory, the demand for military aircraft, including the Avenger, skyrocketed. This was compounded by requests from the Royal Navy for the big, new torpedo bomber, which was well suited for antisubmarine work. Given the impact that U-boat attacks were having on convoys carrying goods to bolster the defense of England, antisubmarine work was considerably important.

Although Grumman's rate of production was soaring—the company would turn out 646 Avengers in 1942, along with scores of F4F Wildcats, which was soon to be supplanted by the bigger, more powerful F6F Hellcat—more capacity was needed.

In order to satisfy the demand, the Navy ordered license-built copies of the TBF-1 from the Eastern Aircraft Division of General Motors.

Eastern Aircraft had been created on January 21, 1942, specifically to build copies of the TBF Avenger and F4F Wildcat, the latter designated FM. Several General Motors plants were included in the Eastern Aircraft Division.

General Motors received a letter of intent concerning Avenger production on February 5, 1942, and four days later a similar letter for Wildcat production. The first contract for the GM-built Avengers, which were designated TBM, was placed on March 23, 1942. Supplements to that contract followed, until the total reached a whopping 1,200 examples, with production scheduled to begin in November 1942.

Eastern's principal locations were the Linden Assembly Plant in Linden New Jersey, and the Trenton-Ternstedt hardware plant in Trenton, New Jersey. These were augmented by the former Delco-Remy Battery plant in Bloomfield, New Jersey, and the former Fisher Body plants in Baltimore, Maryland, and Tarrytown, New York.

TBM assembly would take place in the former Ternstedt plant, which had to be significantly reconditioned for its new role. Work on the remodeling in Trenton began on February 27 and was completed by mid-July. In addition to remodeling the building, provisions had to be made to get the bombers, when completed, out of the building, across a highway as well as the Reading Railroad tracks, and to the nearby Skillman airfield for flight testing.

With the Avenger seeing fleet service, areas needing improvement were quickly identified. By mid-1943, the most significant of these initial improvements began to be incorporated, resulting in new model designations both for Grumman and Eastern aircraft: TBF-1C and TBM-1C, respectively. The models with the suffix *-1C* differed chiefly in eliminating the cowl-mounted .30-caliber machine gun, with forward armament becoming a pair of .50-caliber machine guns, one mounted in each wing, just outside the propeller arc. At the same time, provision was made for carrying a pair of underwing drop tanks, and the radio antenna was relocated. Grumman would build 764 of the TBF-1C, the final production version of the Avenger that the firm would build. Eastern Aircraft would carry the burden of Avenger production alone, although Grumman remained the prime contractor and thus was responsible for all engineering improvements. Eastern would build 2,332 TBM-1C Avengers. Great Britain received 334 of the -1C aircraft. Assorted subvariants of the TBF/TBM-1C were created, as outlined in the following pages.

The second XTBF-1 prototype is parked at the Grumman Aircraft plant at Bethpage, Long Island, on a winter day. The tube protruding from the fuselage just aft of the rectangular window for the radio operator and bombardier's compartment is the fairlead for a trailing wire antenna. *Leo Polaski collection*

Grumman / General Motors Eastern Aircraft Division TBF-1/TBM-1 Avenger Specifications

Wingspan: 54 feet, 2 inches
Length: 40 feet
Height: 16 feet, 5 inches
Empty weight: 10,080 pounds
Maximum weight: 15,900 pounds
Crew: 3
Maximum speed: 271 mph at 12,000 feet
Service ceiling: 22,400 feet
Maximum range: 1,215 miles laden; 1,450 miles unladen
Power plant: One 1,700 hp Wright R-2600-8 Cyclone 14-cylinder, air-cooled radial engine
Armament: One cowl-mounted, .30-caliber Browning machine gun with 300 rounds; one turret-mounted, .50-caliber Browning M2 machine gun with 400 rounds; and one ventral-mounted, .30-caliber Browning machine gun with 500 rounds One 22.4-inch Bliss-Leavitt Mk. 13 torpedo, or maximum of 2,000 pounds of bombs, or depth charges in bomb bay

The Grumman TBF-1 was the first production model of the Avenger torpedo bomber. The early-production TBF-1s were virtually identical to the XTBF-1 second prototype as fitted with the fillet on the rear fuselage. The TBF-1 model continued the practice of having two cowl flaps on the upper quadrants of the rear of the cowling, and two more cowl flaps flanking the lower center of the cowling. All cowl flaps are open in this photo. *National Archives*

The early TBF-1s had the same arrangement of small windows for the radio operator and bombardier's compartment as the XTBF-1 prototypes. Red and white stripes were painted on the rudder. The national insignia were the prewar type, with white stars on blue circles, with a red circle at the center. The dark shape under the canopy to the rear of the front cockpit is the pilot's turnover structure. *National Archives*

The folding wings of the production TBF-1s continued the design initiated with the XTBF-1s, with the wing turning on two separate axes as it was rotated, leading edge pointing down and the wing swinging to the rear. The location of the pitot tube mast on the wingtip is clearly shown here. *National Archives*

In a rear view of an early TBF-1, the .50-caliber machine gun in the turret is visible to the right of center. This allowed the gun to be fired at enemy aircraft that were dead astern, but an interrupter mechanism prevented the machine gun from shooting up the TBF's tail. *National Archives*

This early-production TBF-1 is observed from the front with the cowl flaps open. The Curtiss Electric propellers of the XTBF-1s had been replaced by the Hamilton Standard Hydromatic constant-speed three-blade propeller. This would remain the propeller for all subsequent models of the TBF/TBM Avenger. *National Archives*

The same early TBF-1 is seen from the front with the wings folded. Inside the cowling is a Wright R-2600-8 radial engine, rated at 1,700 horsepower. The two exhaust stacks are protruding from the cowling. *National Archives*

The layout of the pilot's cockpit included the following: *lower left*, the throttle quadrant; *to the front*, the main instrument panel, sliding chart board below the main panel, and additional controls and instruments; and, *to the lower right*, the electrical panel and circuit breakers. *National Archives*

This photo was the basis for an illustration of the left side of the pilot's cockpit in the TBF-1 pilot's manual. The seat had a built-in armrest on each side. To the rear of the sidewall of the cockpit were the map case and the SBAE (Stabilized Bombing Approach Equipment: part of the Norden bombsight system) attitude control, over a console containing the tailwheel caster lock and controls for the trim tabs. Farther forward was the throttle quadrant, containing the control levers for the throttle, supercharger, and fuel mixture. Above the throttle quadrant is a fluorescent light. *National Archives*

To the right of the pilot's seat was a console, on the top of which was the electrical distribution panel and on the side of which were electrical breakers. On the rear of the sidewall were clips for storing flares, and two T-handles for releasing parachute flares.

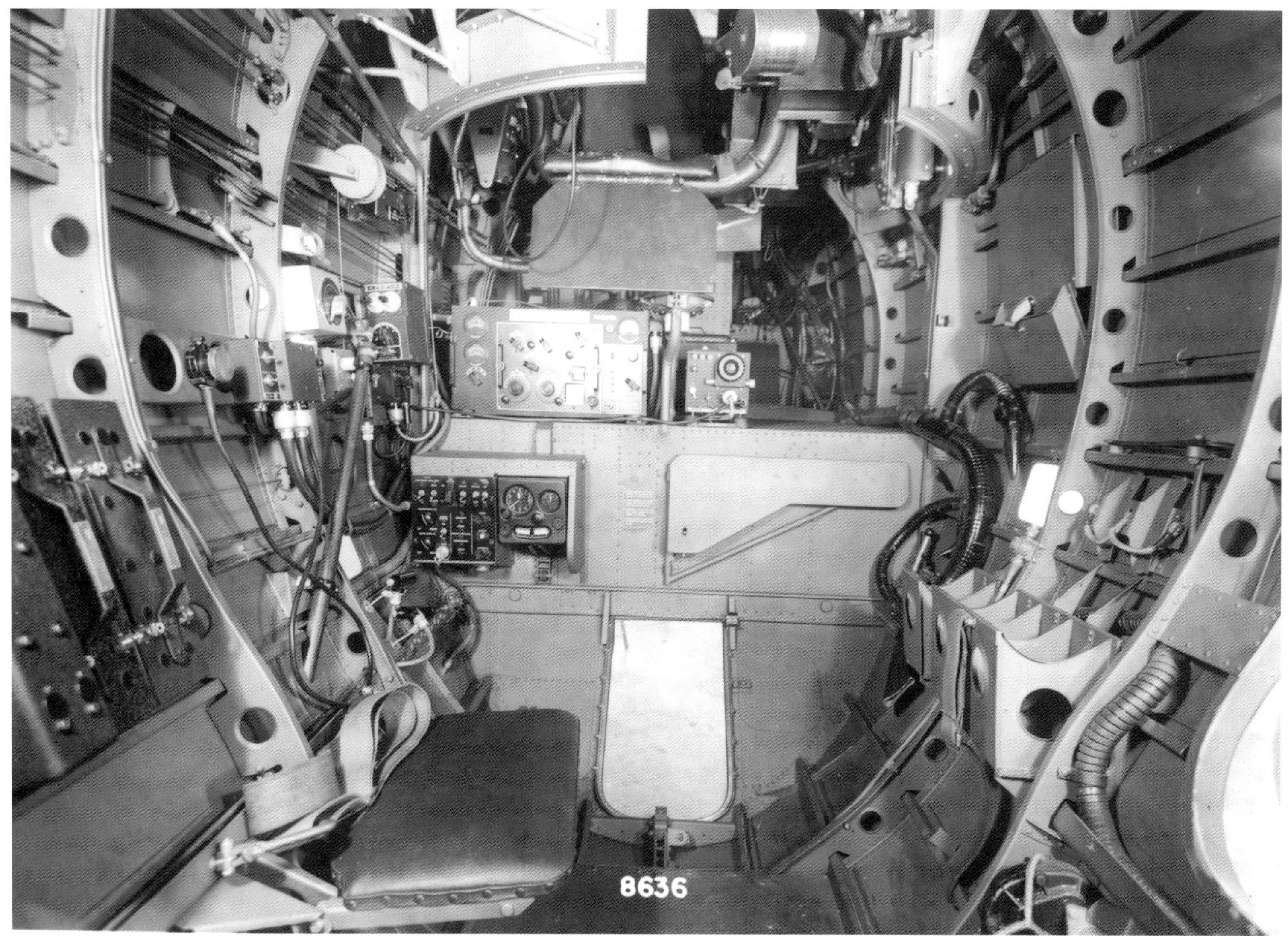

The radio operator and bombardier's compartment of the early-production TBF-1s had a folding bench seat on the left side. At the front of the compartment was a bulkhead separating this space from the bomb bay; an aiming window for a Norden bombsight (not installed here) was on the center of the bulkhead. To the upper left of the window are the bombardier's electrical panel and instrument panel, above which are radio equipment and the lower part of the turret. Above the window on the bulkhead was a folding table. *Leo Polaski collection*

During production of the TBF-1, there were revisions to the radio operator and bombardier's compartment. The windows were redesigned, and the seat was changed to fold down across the compartment, rather than against the left sidewall. A telegraph key is attached to the folding table above the bomb-aiming window. *National Archives*

The new folding seat introduced during TBF-1 production is seen from another angle. On the side of the fuselage to the immediate front of the seat were bombing controls and equipment for the trailing antenna, including the antenna reel. *National Archives*

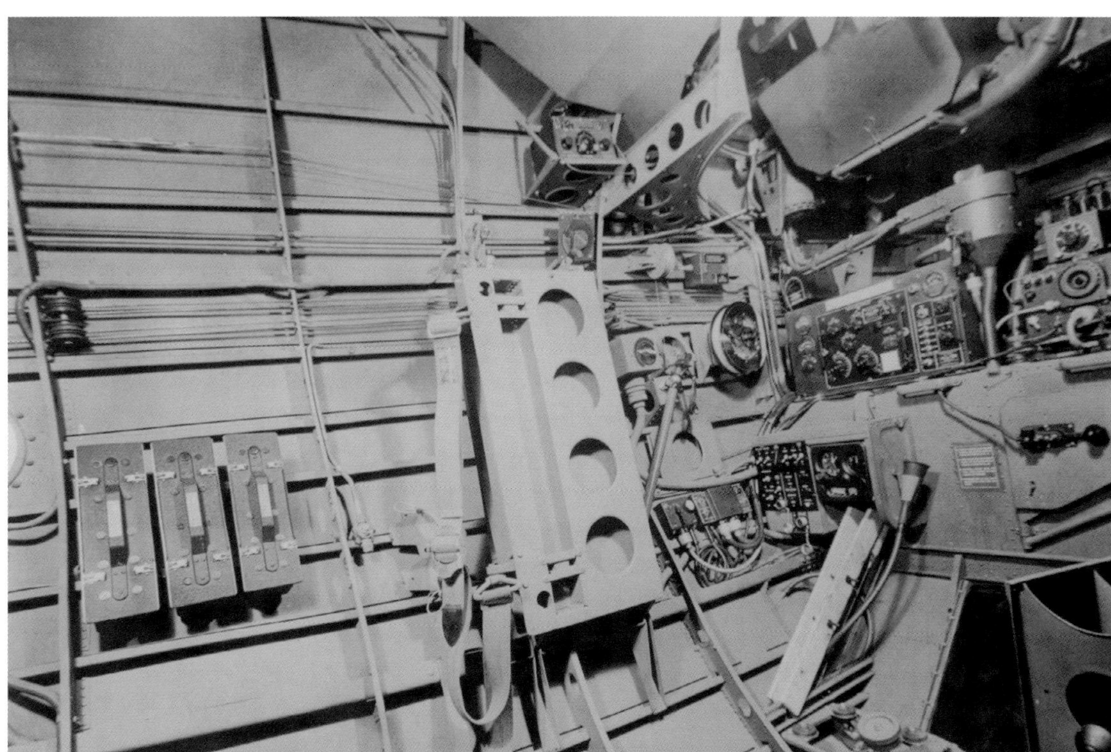

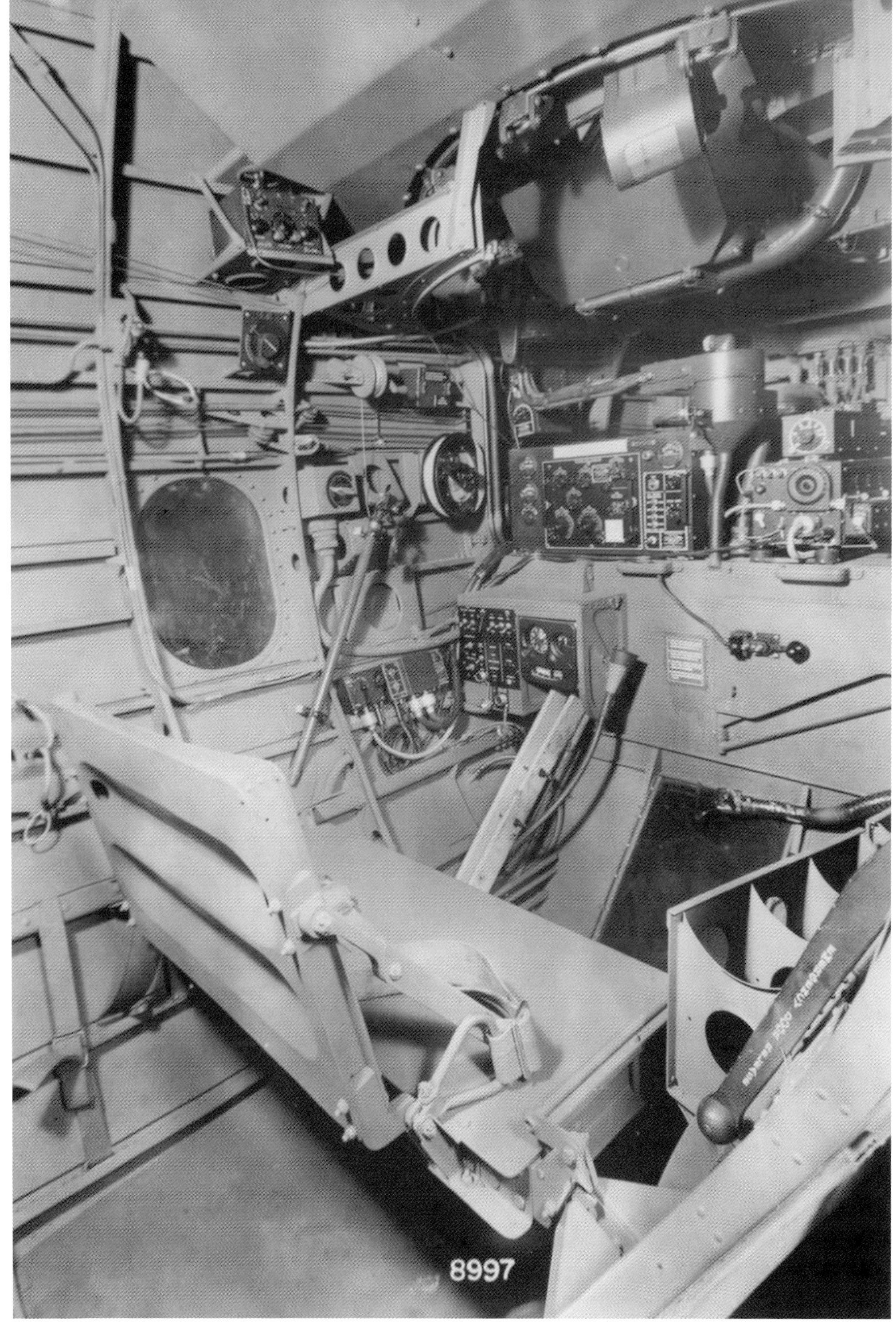

The radio operator and bombardier's compartment of a later TBF-1 is seen through the access door, showing the seat folded down. To the lower right is the emergency release for that door. The lower part of the turret is to the upper right. *National Archives*

The TBF-1, as well as later Avengers, was equipped to carry bombs in its weapons bay, in addition to torpedoes. In fact, it has been reported that Avengers delivered bombs to targets with much more frequency than torpedoes. Shown here is a TBF-1 with two bombs about to be hoisted to the racks in the bay. *Leo Polaski collection*

A detachment of Torpedo Squadron 8 (VT-8) was the first Navy unit to receive the new TBF-1s, in early 1942. Here, crewmen are preparing to fly one of the TBF-1s assigned to VT-8 to Naval Air Station (NAS) Norfolk, Virginia. The crewman on the wing is about to enter the aft cockpit, which was fitted with flight controls in the first 50 TBF-1s. *Stan Piet collection*

The same TBF-1, assigned to VT-8, is seen with wings folded. Soon after delivery to NAS Norfolk, the red and white stripes on the rudder would be painted over. *Leo Polaski collection*

An early-production Grumman TBF-1 is observed from the left side in early 1942. Note the recessed step with a curved top in the fuselage below the rectangular window in the radio operator and bombardier's compartment, and the angled line with an arrow at the bottom to help crewmen discern the step. Jutting from the fuselage just below the turret is a grab handle. *Leo Polaski collection*

One of the earliest TBF-1s flies off a coastline in early 1942. The camouflage scheme was the one authorized for aircraft carrier planes on October 31, 1941, consisting of NS Blue Gray over NS Light Gray. *Stan Piet collection*

The national insignia authorized on May 6, 1942, with the red circle removed from the center, has been applied to this TBF-1. The nonslip panel on the wing next to the fuselage was black next to the pilot's cockpit and a lighter shade to the trailing edge of the wing. *Stan Piet collection*

The same TBF-1 shown in the preceding photo is viewed from another perspective. Faintly visible in the two photos of the plane are the redesigned windows for the radio operator and bombardier's compartment, introduced after TBF-1 production got underway. This evidently was a test or ferrying flight, since the aircraft is unarmed and no unit markings are present. *Leo Polaski collection*

This Avenger is identifiable as a TBF-1 by the position of the backward-angled radio antenna mast to the immediate rear of the pilot's sliding canopy, and the presence of a trough on the top of the cowling to allow firing clearance for a fixed .30-caliber machine gun. The round window was omitted from the door of the radio operator and bombardier's compartment after production of the TBF-1s began. *Leo Polaski collection*

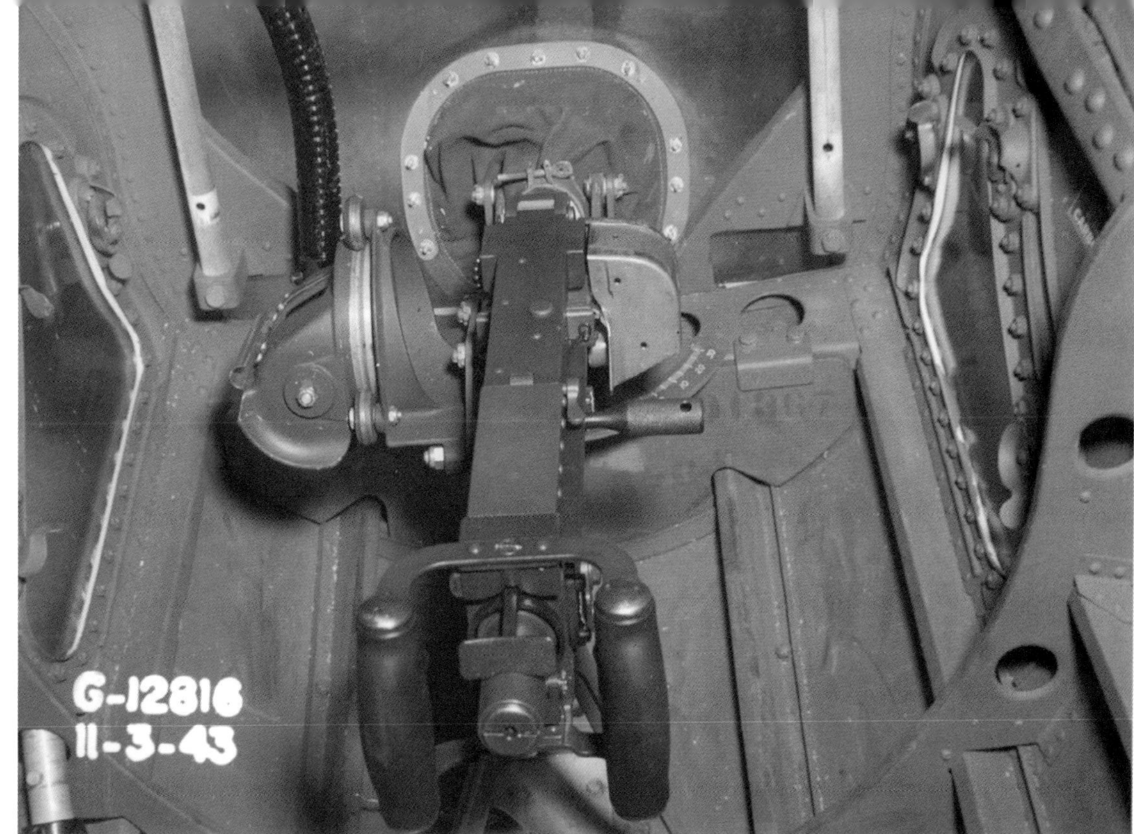

The .30-caliber belly "stinger" machine gun is viewed up close in a TBF-1 in a photo dated November 3, 1943. Mounted in a space called the "tunnel," the gun was equipped with twin grips, an ammunition feed assembly on the left, and a spent-casing deflector on the right side of the receiver. The triangular side windows were removable and were held in place by three cam locks. Part of an azimuth or deflection scale is visible below the spent-casing deflector. The two vertical, light-colored tubes to the sides of the gun are stanchions for a sliding armored shield, which was out of view in the raised position when this photo was taken. *National Archives*

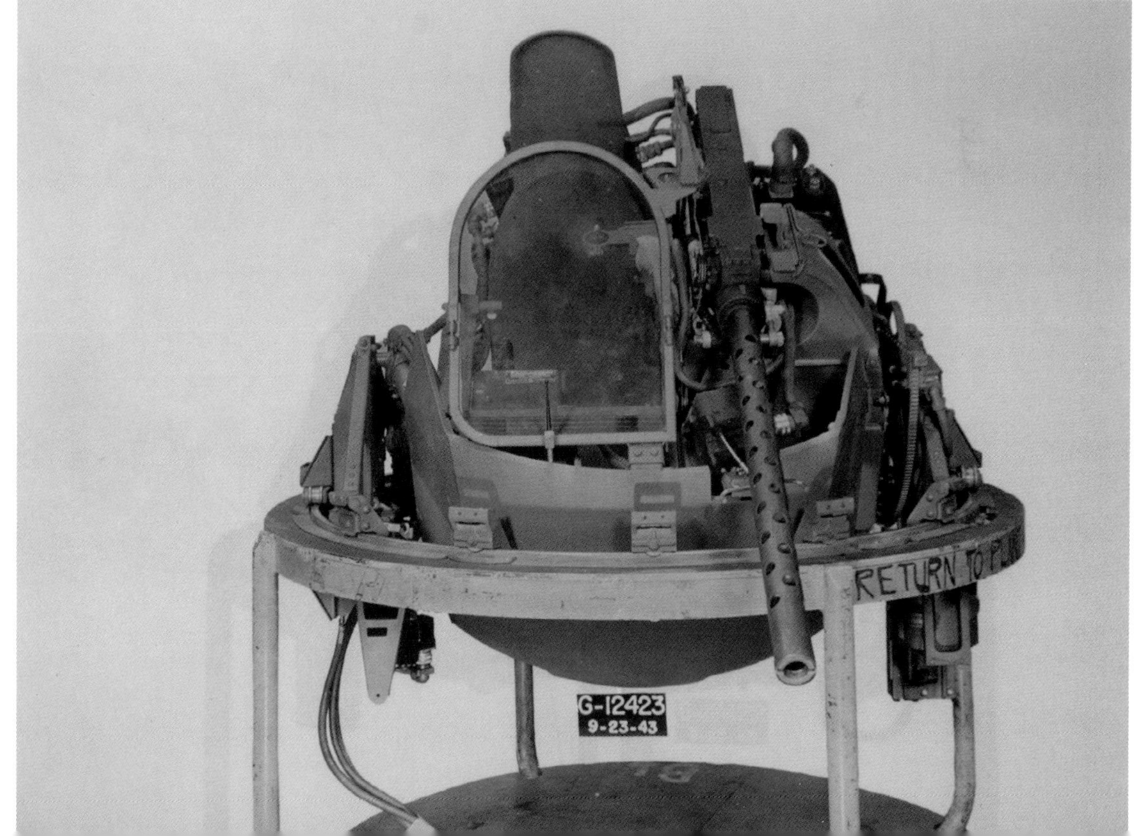

As seen in a September 23, 1943, photo of a unit mounted on a stand, the turret of the TBF-1 and subsequent models of Avengers was designed by Grumman and carried the model numbers 150SE-1 and 150SE-2. It was an amplidyne electric, ball-type design and was armed with a single Browning .50-caliber machine gun. For protection, the gunner was provided with an armored shield and a piece of ballistic glass to the front, and armor to the rear of his seat. *National Archives*

The Grumman turret is seen from the right side with the machine gun dismounted. The armored shield had extensions on the sides. Trunnions on each side of the gun mount rested on triangular supports, allowing the gunner's seat, shield, and machine gun to elevate as a unit. The mount was installed on a circular race, for traversing. *National Archives*

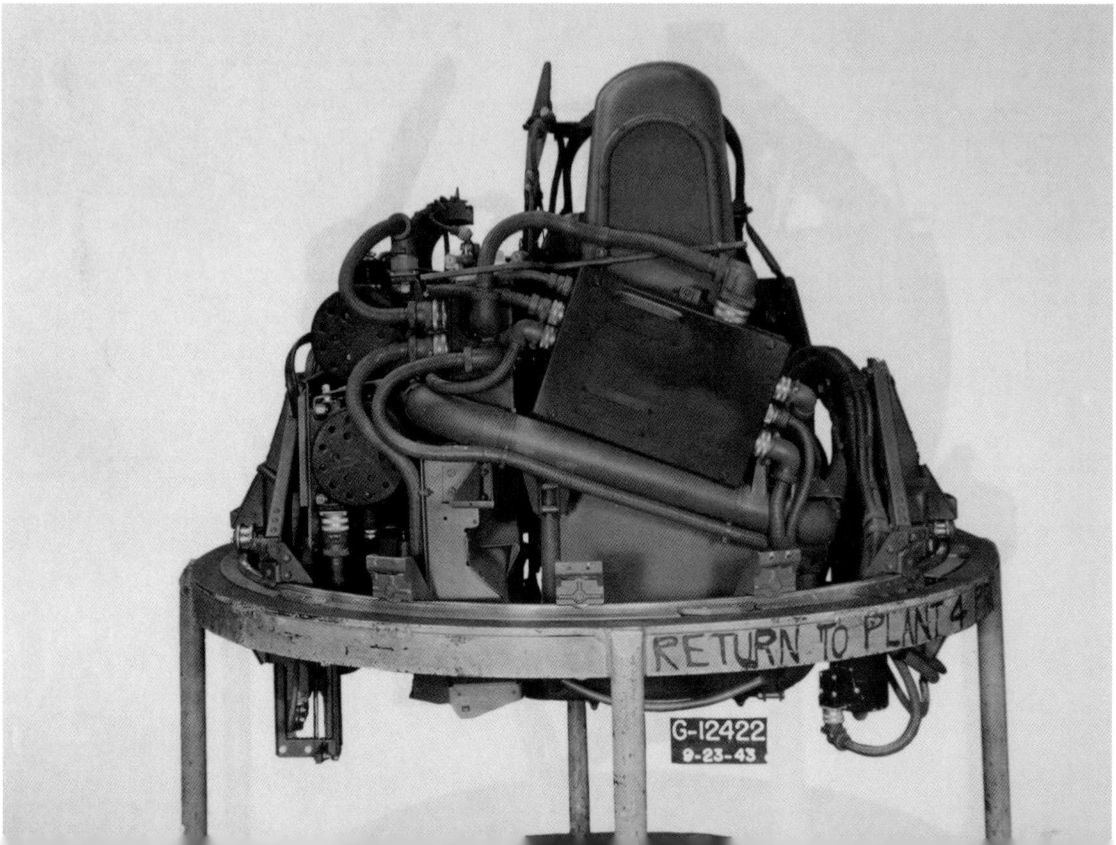

The turret is viewed from the rear, at 0-degree elevation, with the Plexiglas dome removed, showing the electrical junction box on the rear of the seat, electrical conduits, the tubular support frame, the turret ring, and the trunnion supports. *National Archives*

Grumman completed 646 Avengers in 1942, but during that year the Navy determined that Grumman's priority during the next year must be the production of the new F6F Hellcat fighter. Thus, to free up production at Grumman, the Navy contracted with the Eastern Aircraft Division of General Motors to produce Avengers, beginning with the TBM-1, basically identical to the TBF-1. Shown here is one of the Eastern TBM-1s in flight. Eastern completed 550 of them, BuNos 24521 to 25070. *Stan Piet collection*

In late 1942 and early 1943, the United States began transferring Avengers to the British under the Lend-Lease Program. Initially the British designated these aircraft, based on the TBF-1, the Tarpon Mk. I, but in January 1944 they changed the name to Avenger Mk. I. In this photo, a Royal Navy Tarpon Mk. I cruising above Long Island Sound in 1943 bears a camouflage scheme of Extra Dark Sea Grey and Dark Slate Grey over Sky Type S paint.

A Tarpon Mk. I destined for the Royal Navy's Fleet Air Arm has been prepared for shipment by removing the outer wings and empennage, covering the airframe with sealant, and mounting it on a stand. The dome-shaped window on the radio operator and bombardier's compartment was one of the customizations the British made to their Tarpons. *Leo Polaski collection*

A crewman is mounting a Tarpon/Avenger Mk. I, Royal Navy serial number FN795 and code C27. This aircraft formerly was USN BuNo 47487. Blackburn Aircraft installed British modifications on Tarpons, to include dome windows on the radio operator and bombardier's compartment, oxygen systems and gunsights, and fitting out a navigator's compartment in the second cockpit. *Imperial War Museum*

The Grumman TBF-1C and Eastern TBM-1C took the TBF-1/TBM-1 airframe and implemented several revisions, the most noticeable of which was the elimination of the .30-caliber machine gun to the front of the windscreen and the installation of a .50-caliber machine gun in each wing. The port for the left .50-caliber machine gun is faintly visible on the leading edge of the wing of this TBM-1C from Composite Squadron 42 (VC-42) in November 1943. Although a radio mast relocated aft from its original position and mounted in a vertical rather than raked-back attitude is considered another key feature of the -1C, this example has the mast as originally arranged. Under the wing is a Yagi radar antenna, an innovation that gave USN aircraft such as the Avenger a much-enhanced navigational ability. A flame damper has been fitted over the exhaust on this example. *National Museum of Naval Aviation*

The absence of the trough in the cowling for the now-omitted fixed machine gun is noticeable in this photo of TBF-1C number 5 from VT-18 over the South Pacific on August 12, 1944. The TBF/TBM-1Cs retained the two upper and two lower cowl flaps of the TBF/TBM-1. Four zero-length stub launchers for rockets and a Yagi radar antenna are under the right wing. *National Museum of Naval Aviation*

The access doors for the .50-caliber machine gun (*left*) and the ammunition box (*right*) are open on this right outer-wing section of a TBF/TBM-1C. A blister was incorporated into the door for the machine gun to allow clearance for the rear of the gun's receiver. *National Archives*

When an ASD-1 radar set was installed in a radome on the leading edge of the right wing of the TBF/TBM-1, the aircraft was given the suffix *-1D*. Similar installations on TBF-1C airframes were designated TBF-1CD. The example pictured here, apparently a TBF-1CD on the basis of the angle and position of the antenna mast, was serving with VT-51, based on USS *San Jacinto* (CVL-30) in July 1944. *Naval History and Heritage Command*

A TBF/TBM-1D or TBF-1CD is viewed from the front, showing the position of the ASD-1 radar. This was an airborne, microwave-search and torpedo-laying radar for locating and tracking surface craft and coastal targets, as well as for general navigation, blind bombing, and torpedo laying. It could detect, for example, surfaced submarines at up to 20 miles and well-defined coastlines at 80 miles. *Tailhook Association*

The top of the radome is visible on the right wing of a TBM-1D or TBF-1CD at NAS Patuxent River, Maryland, in 1944. Eight zero-length rocket launchers are under the wings, and Yagi radar antennas are in an unusual position on the tops of the wings. *Tailhook Association*

In addition to Avengers equipped with leading-edge radome pods, some were fitted with underwing radar pods, such as this TBF-1C, side number 707 and BuNo 45707, photographed at NAS Patuxent River, Maryland, in 1944. Note the new, recessed handhold on the fuselage below the turret. *Tailhook Association*

CHAPTER 3

TBM-3

While the replacement of the single forward-firing .30-caliber machine gun with a pair of the much more potent .50-caliber machine guns solved much of one of the Avenger's major problems, it actually made another worse. The TBF-1C was considerably heavier than its predecessor, and many pilots already felt that the big Grumman was underpowered.

Resolving to solve this problem, Grumman first considered installing a Pratt & Whitney R-2800, but that engine was in short supply owing to the demands for Thunderbolt, Hellcat, and Corsair production. Instead, the company turned to an uprated version of the engine already powering the Avenger—the R-2600-20. This engine was rated at 1,900 horsepower, 200 more than the R-2600-8 powering Avengers thus far. Grumman built two XTBF-3 prototypes, along with a single XTBF-2 prototype, powered by a R-2600-10 engine and boasting a two-stage supercharger.

The Grumman prototypes were followed by two General Motors XTBM-3 prototypes. With the concept proven, Eastern began to turn out the TBM-3 en masse, while Grumman ceased series production of the Avenger, concentrating instead on the Hellcat. Despite the Eastern Aircraft Division of General Motors now becoming the sole source for series-production Avengers, production of the torpedo bomber continued to climb, with monthly production peaking at 400 aircraft in March 1945. Ultimately, 4,657 TBM-3s and variants were manufactured.

The TBM-3s could be distinguished from their predecessors by the double cowl-mounted cooling intakes (the -1 and -1C have only one at the top) and more-numerous and larger cowl flaps, needed for proper cooling of the more powerful engine.

Beneath the TBM-3's wings were zero-length rocket stubs, and inside the cockpit the pilot's instrument panel was redesigned, becoming flat across its top.

The TBM-3 would be adapted for a variety of roles. A night-bomber variant, the TBM-3D, was created by modifying existing TBM-3 aircraft through the installation of ASD-1 radar, with the radome being fitted to the leading edge of the right wing and the primary radarscope being installed in the radio compartment. A smaller secondary radarscope was installed in the cockpit. To reduce weight, the ventral gun as well as some of the armor plate was removed, it being felt that the cover of darkness would help protect the aircrew. Relatively few aircraft were modified to TBM-3D configuration.

The TBM-3E, introduced in late 1944, was factory produced and boasted a stronger airframe that was, incredibly, 1 ton lighter than its predecessor, which certainly helped the power-to-weight ratio.

First flying on August 5, 1944, the TBM-3W featured a powerful surface-search radar mounted beneath the fuselage. The program leading to the development of this aircraft was Project Cadillac, named not for the car but for Maine's Cadillac Mountain, where sun first hits the US in the morning. In order to install the radar system, all weapons were removed from the Avenger, including the turret, and a rear canopy was installed to accommodate the two radar operators. Small fins were added to the tailplane to offset the effect of the bulbous radome extending below the fuselage. The war ended before the TBM-3W could be deployed, but forty of the conversions were approved, and the type operated postwar. Subsequently, an improved version, the TBM-3W2, was developed for antisubmarine work, and in such a role it was teamed with the TBM-3S, which dispensed with the normal Avenger turret but featured a searchlight, a radar of its own, and a data link to couple it to the powerful TBM-3W2 radar equipment. About 160 aircraft were converted to TBM-3W2 configuration, while an unknown quantity became TBM-3S.

Early in the Korean War, with the Avenger becoming obsolete as a combat aircraft, some TBM-3 and TBM-3E aircraft were stripped of their armor and armament to become transport aircraft capable of delivering personnel and equipment to aircraft carriers at sea. These aircraft were known as TBM-3R.

Solely produced by Eastern Aircraft at Trenton, New Jersey, the TBM-3 came about out of the necessity to provide more power to the Avenger. Although the engine selected, the Wright R-2600-20 Twin Cyclone, produced 1,900 horsepower—200 more than the R-2600-8 used in the earlier models of Avenger—the gains in speed were negated by the increased weight of the plane. As seen in this photo of TBM-3s, the number and size of cowl flaps were increased on this model. *National Archives*

Prior to committing to TBM-3 production, two TBF-1s, BuNos 24141 and 24341, were converted to XTBF-3s by mounting Wright R-2600-20 engines in them. One of these two planes is shown in this photo: the first three digits of the BuNo appear to be 241, which would make it the first XTBF-3. *National Museum of Naval Aviation*

A Wright R-2600-20 radial engine is suspended from hoist chains and a sling on the assembly line, showing details of the ignition harness, the black pushrods and rocker covers, and the dome-shaped gear-reduction housing with a data plate affixed to the side. *National Archives*

As seen from the right side, an R-2600-20 is installed on its engine mount, ready for installation in a TBM-3 Avenger. The prominent protrusion on the lower front of the gear-reduction housing contained the crankcase front-section oil pump and oil pump strainer. *National Archives*

An R-2600-20 engine unit is viewed from the right, showing, *from front to rear*: the propeller shaft, gear-reduction housing, cowling ring with intakes for the carburetor (*top*) and oil cooler (*bottom*), cylinders, right exhaust, fireproof bulkhead, and rear of the engine support, attached to a trolley. *National Archives*

The pilot's instrument panel in the TBM-3 was of a different design than those of preceding models of the Avenger, featuring a nearly flat top and a different assortment and positioning of the instruments. A sliding chart board remained in place below the instrument panel. A gunsight is on the top of the panel. *National Archives*

The left side of the pilot's cockpit of the TBM-3 retained the throttle quadrant and the side console of preceding models, adding an arrestor-hook control lever to the top of the console in place of the formerly used switch below the console for operating the hook. The SBAE attitude control above the console had been discontinued. *National Archives*

The right subpanel and console of a TBM-3 are displayed. On the subpanel were several gauges and the gun-charger control. Above the console were radio controls. *National Archives*

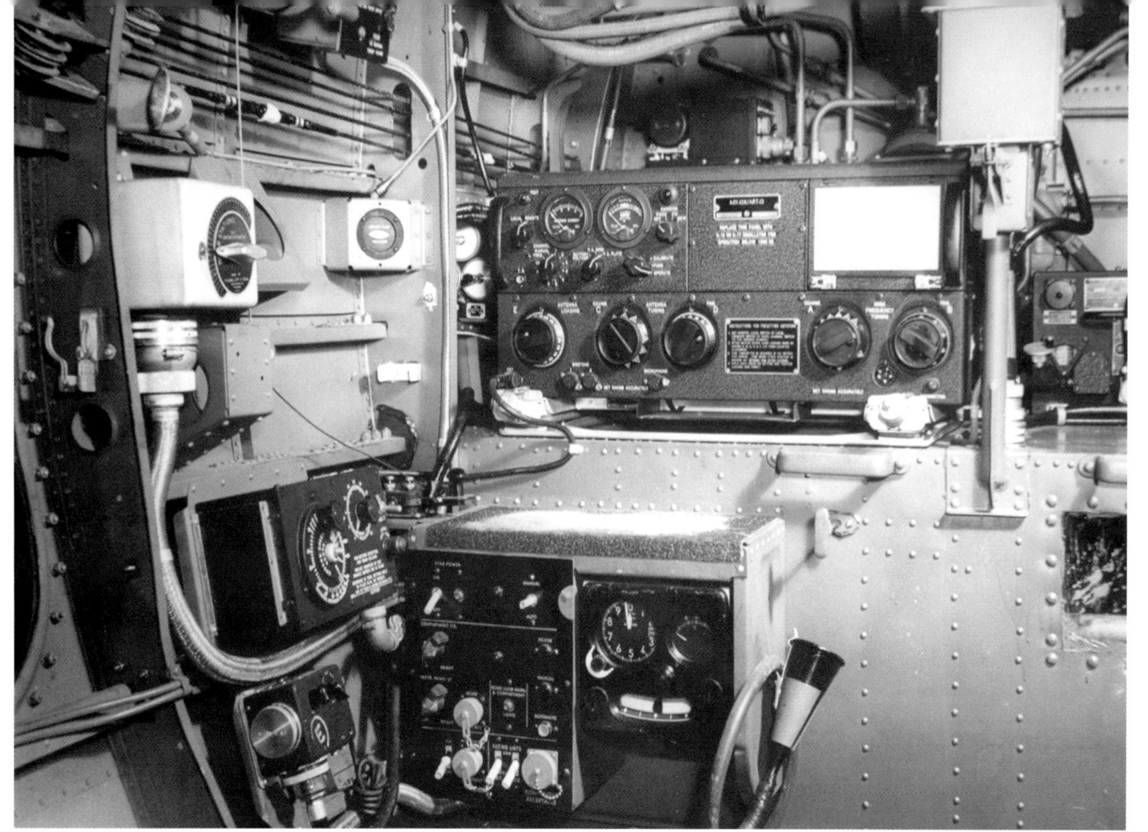

The left front corner of the radio operator and bombardier's compartment of a TBM-3 is shown. On the floor below the turret is the radio receiver, below which is the bombardier's panel. Clipped to the side of the bombardier's panel is a relief tube. On the sidewall to the left are items such as an oxygen-flow indicator, bomb selector, and intervalometer for controlling the time between the release of bombs. *National Archives*

Looking forward from the right side of the radio operator and bombardier's compartment, the passageway past the turret and into the rear cockpit, in which radio equipment was stored, is in the center background. In the right foreground is a bracket for a radar scope. *National Archives*

The second cockpit of the Avenger was converted into a storage space for radio and radar equipment starting with the TBF/TBM-1C. This included removing the seat, instruments, and flight controls. This photo, taken from the right side of the second cockpit of a TBM-3, shows an ARB radio receiver and rack in the left side of the space. *National Archives*

The torpedo and bomb bay of a TBM-3 is viewed from the forward end facing aft, showing hoisting cables, bomb racks to the sides, torpedo racks and sway braces to the top, and the open bay door to the side. *National Archives*

Twelve 100-pound bombs are installed on the racks in the torpedo and bomb bay of a TBM-3. Other types and sizes of bombs, including depth bombs for antisubmarine operations, could be carried on the racks. *National Archives*

The twelve 100-pound bombs in the TBM-3 are viewed from a different angle. A solid panel has been placed over the bomb-sighting window on the bulkhead at the rear of the bay. *National Archives*

In a view of the interior of the turret of a TBM-3 with the side access door removed, to the lower right is the grip by which the gunner controlled the traverse, elevation, and firing of the .50-caliber machine gun. To the front of the grip is a panel of bulletproof glass. To the front of that glass is the ring sight; to the rear of the glass is the gunsight. Above the gunsight is a bracket for a gun camera. *National Archives*

A view of the turret from farther forward shows, *from bottom to top*, the trunnion to the gunner's right, the control grip, the ring sight, and the bulletproof glass panel. *National Archives*

The .50-caliber machine gun in the right wing is displayed with the access panel removed. The sticker on the interior of the access panel reads, "FASTEN DOOR BEFORE SPREADING WING." *National Archives*

Tri-State Warbird Museum, Batavia, Ohio, preserves this TBM-3 Avenger, BuNo 53420 and manufacturer's serial number 3482; it flies under civil registration number NL420GP. The United States transferred this Avenger to the Royal Canadian Navy in October 1950, and it later performed as a fire-fighting aircraft. *Rich Kolasa*

In a view of TBM-3, BuNo 53420, details of the restored turret, canopy, and radio operator and bombardier's compartment windows are available. The whip antenna on the canopy was a postwar addition. *Rich Kolasa*

Eastern Aircraft TBM-3, BuNo 53638 and manufacturer's serial number 3700, was another Avenger transferred to the Royal Canadian Navy in the early 1950s, and another postwar alumnus of Conair Ltd. The plane has been restored and painted in tricolor camouflage. It now bears civil registration number N109K and is in the collection of the Mid-Atlantic Air Museum, Reading, Pennsylvania. *Rich Kolasa*

A left-front view of TBM-3, BuNo 53638, includes details of the Hamilton Standard Hydromatic propeller; the cowling, cowl flaps, and left exhaust; the left torpedo and bomb bay door; and the windscreen and canopy. *Rich Kolasa*

As was the practice on Navy aircraft in World War II, "NAVY" over the Bureau Number, 53638, are stenciled in small figures on the dorsal fin, while the plane's nomenclature, "TBM-3," is stenciled on the upper part of the rudder. As was the case of many Avengers that served as firefighters after World War II, the windows for the tunnel machine gun have been removed, and this part of the fuselage has not been restored. *Rich Kolasa*

Some features of the wing-fold joint, the upper part of the right main landing gear, and the fuselage and cowling on TBM-3, BuNo 53638, are in view. Note the bare-metal clamp that holds the elbow of the exhaust in place. *Rich Kolasa*

Charles Lynch, of White Plains, New York, is the owner of this restored TBM-3, BuNo 53835 and civil registration number N3967A. *Rich Kolasa*

General Motors Eastern Aircraft Division TBM-3 Avenger Specifications

Wingspan: 54 feet, 2 inches
Length: 40 feet
Height: 16 feet, 5 inches
Empty weight: 10,843 pounds
Maximum weight: 18,250 pounds
Crew: 3
Maximum speed: 267 mph at 16,000 feet
Service ceiling: 23,400 feet
Maximum range: 1,130 miles laden; 1,920 miles unladen
Power plant: One 1,900 hp Wright R-2600-20 Cyclone 14-cylinder, air-cooled radial engine
Armament: Two wing-mounted, .50-caliber Browning machine guns with 300 rounds; one turret-mounted, .50-caliber Browning M2 machine gun with 400 rounds; and one ventral-mounted, .30-caliber Browning machine gun with 500 rounds One 22.4-inch Bliss-Leavitt Mk. 13 torpedo, or maximum of 2,000 pounds of bombs, or depth charges in bomb bay

The external arrestor hook seen on surviving TBM-3s was actually a feature of late-production TBM-3Es. Below the front cockpit is a commemorative sticker for the Naval Aviation Centennial. A bomb rack is mounted under the wing to the rear of the main landing-gear bay. In this restoration, the tunnel machine gun mount and the triangular side windows were omitted. *Rich Kolasa*

Two oblong, Plexiglas access panels are on the side of the turret. The second cockpit of the TBM-3, as well as other models of the Avenger, had a clamshell hatch that could be entered or exited from the right side only. The hatch consisted of the top and right-side sections of the canopy, joined by piano hinges. *Rich Kolasa*

A radar-equipped version of the TBM-3 for night-bombing operations was produced, the TBM-3D. It had the ASD-1 radar, with the radome fitted on the leading edge of the right outer wing. The TBM-3Ds typically served with night torpedo-bomber squadrons, such as VT(N)-90, which was assigned to USS *Enterprise* (CV-6) after that carrier was repurposed as a night carrier. *Tailhook Association*

TBM-3Ds often were armed with 5-inch rockets on zero-length launchers, as well as a searchlight in a pod mounted under the left wing, as seen in a photo of BuNo 23506. The searchlight pod had a clear Plexiglas dome on the front to allow the light to shine through. The plane is painted in the USN tricolor camouflage scheme of Sea Blue, Intermediate Blue, and Insignia White. The number "506" likely was applied by the manufacturer before delivery to the Navy. *Tailhook Association*

Part of the forward portion of a center-wing assembly for a TBM-3D is pictured before the skin is applied, showing the varying shapes of the ribs, which are attached to the main spar. *National Archives*

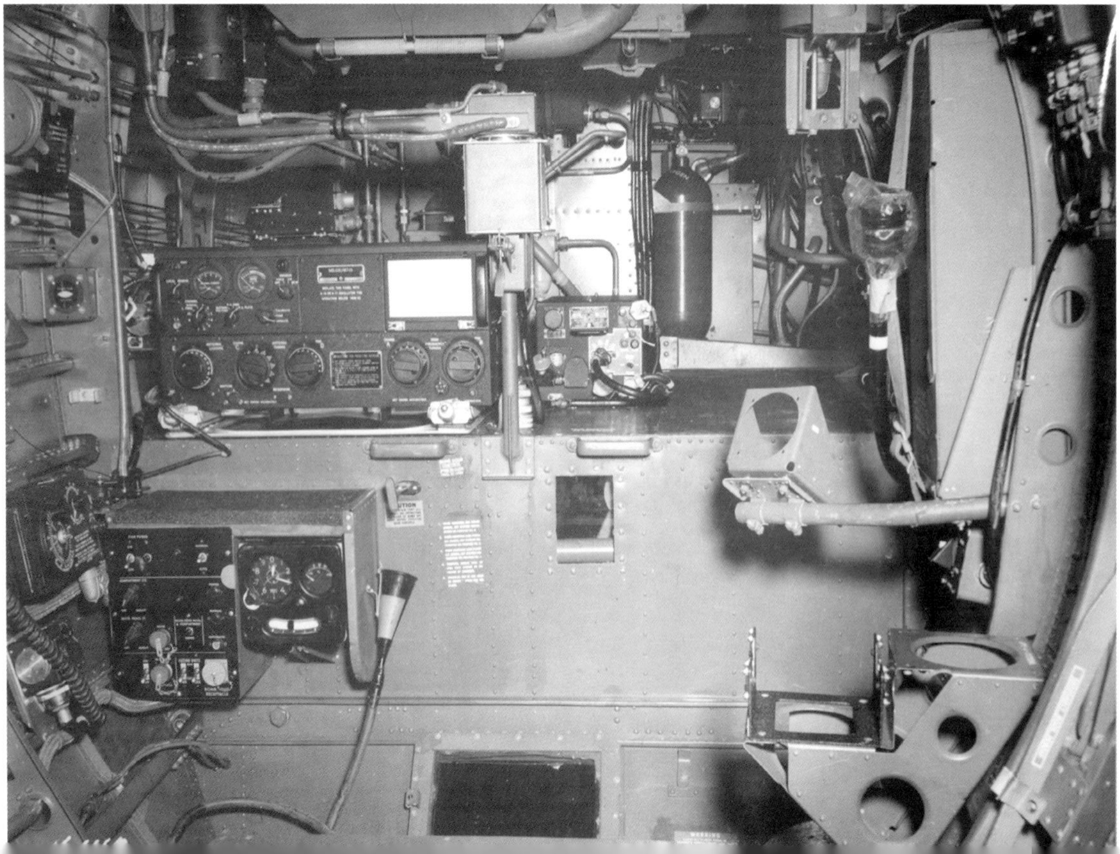

The radio operator and bombardier's compartment of the TBM-3D had a layout virtually the same as that of the TBM-3, pictured earlier. To the right are brackets for a radar scope, also called an indicator unit (mounted on a horizontal tube) and for an indicator amplifier and radar control box (*bottom right*). *National Archives*

The Eastern Aircraft TBM-3E represented an effort to squeeze more efficiency out of the Wright R-2600 engine by lightening the airframe, chiefly by eliminating the .30-caliber machine gun in the tunnel position. The TBM-3E also employed an APS-4 radar, with the radar antenna being located in a pod under the right wing. *National Archives*

Late in TBM-3E production, from BuNo 86175 onward, the internally stored arrestor hook was replaced by an external hook. This was changed because of the tendency of the internal hook to corrode, leading to failures of the hook during landings. *National Archives*

From this angle, with wings folded, the TBM-3E looked much like a TBM-3 or TBM-3D. The number "129" painted on the fuselage was in the style of identification numbers applied by the manufacturer. *National Archives*

The late-war camouflage of overall Glossy Sea Blue of this TBM-3E contrasts with the corrugated-metal factory building in the background. The APS-4 radar pod is visible under the right wing. *National Archives*

TBM-3E, BuNo 85632, manufacturer's construction number 2451, and civil registration number NL81865, is owned by Brad Deckert. The plane was completed in early 1945 and flew with Marine Torpedo Bomber Squadron 234 (VMTB-234) aboard the escort carrier USS *Vella Gulf* (CVE-111) in the Okinawa Campaign. After the war the plane served as a firefighting aircraft and subsequently was restored and was painted in colors and markings for VMTB-234. *Rich Kolasa*

TBM-3E, BuNo 85632, is viewed from the right side during a flight, with the radar pod and a bomb suspended from the wing. Note the gun camera on the two-legged mount to the front of the windscreen. This Avenger has the correct internal arrestor hook for a TBM-3E prior to BuNo 86175. *Rich Kolasa*

Rockets are mounted on zero-length launchers under the wings of TBM-3E, BuNo 85632. The landing gear is in the process of being retracted. *Rich Kolasa*

The TBM-3E is painted in late-war Glossy Sea Blue; however, the frames of the windscreen, canopy, and turret dome are painted matte black. *Rich Kolasa*

TBM-3E, BuNo 85632, is viewed from the left rear, with the radar pod visible under the right wing. *Rich Kolasa*

"Ida Red" is the nickname of this restored TBM-3E, BuNo 85882 and construction number 2701. It flies under civil registration number N9584Z and is painted in antisubmarine camouflage of gray over white. *Rich Kolasa*

A flame damper is on the left exhaust of "Ida Red." Four pairs of zero-length rocket launchers are visible on the underside of the left wing. *Rich Kolasa*

In a photo of "Ida Red" banking right, the mount for an external arrestor hook is visible on the bottom of the tail, aft of the tail landing gear. A bomb rack is on the center wing section. A clear view is available of the letterbox slots on the left wing. *Rich Kolasa*

As seen in a view of the left landing gear, the oleo strut is braced by a side strut and, to the rear, a drag strut. A fairing or door is attached to the inboard side of the oleo strut. The wheels are mounted with size 34 × 9 tires. The triangular panel to the upper right was hinged and serves to cover a notch in the wing that provides clearance during the folding and extension of the wing. This panel operated automatically.

Details of the left main landing-gear bay are displayed. Also in view are two forward zero-length rocket launchers.

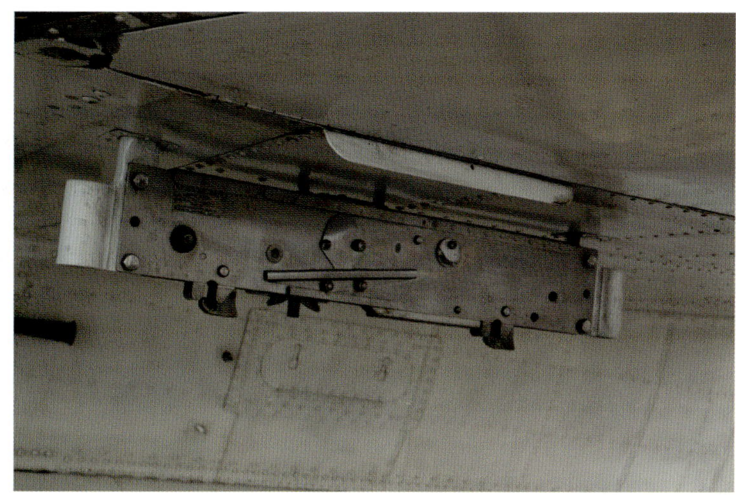

A removable bomb rack was part of the equipment for the TBM-3E; this one is on the left wing of "Ida Red." On the bottom of the unit are the two bomb-carrying hooks. The data plate identifies the rack as made by Pollak Manufacturing Co., Burlington, New Jersey.

The forward end of the right bomb-bay door is displayed in the open position. Each of the two door assemblies was of a clamshell or bifolding design. An actuator arm at each end of the door operated it.

In a view of the right wing, the dark-colored object on the landing-gear door is a hook for attaching the catapult bridle. A similar hook is on the left main landing-gear door.

The left bomb and torpedo bay door and its front actuating arm are displayed. On the lower front of the oleo strut of the main landing gear is the anti-torque link, which acted to keep the wheel parallel to the longitudinal centerline of the aircraft.

Inside the bomb and torpedo bay of "Ida Red," in the foreground are fuel and hydraulic lines and electrical conduits. In the background, a container is secured in the bay. This is not the droppable 275-gallon auxiliary fuel tank that could be installed in the bay.

"Ida Red" is viewed from behind the trailing edge of the right wing. The two grab handles on the side of the fuselage below the canopy appear to be postwar modifications. Below the aft section of canopy is the access door for the life-raft storage container.

Elements in view along the right side of the fuselage include the side of the turret and the two oblong access panels, the recessed grab handle below the turret, the life-raft access door, the canopy, and the nonslip panel on the wing.

As seen in this photo, it is no wonder that aircrews of Avengers referred to the turret by the nickname "the goldfish bowl." The trunnion is visible through the lower Plexiglas access panel on the side of the turret. With the .50-caliber machine gun elevated, the armored shield for the gunner is in view.

The horizontal stabilizers and the vertical fin were of all-metal construction. The rudder and elevators (not shown here) were constructed of aluminum-alloy frames with fabric skin and were statically and dynamically balanced. The rudder had a split tab; the upper part, seen here, was the servo tab, and the lower part was the trim tab.

The tail landing gear of the TBM-3E, as was the case of other models of the Avenger, was hydraulically operated and featured a fully swiveling wheel that could be locked so as not to swivel. Here, the wheel has swiveled 180 degrees; the front of the aircraft is toward the right. A fairing or door is on the front of the gear, while a Bendix shock absorber is on the rear of the gear.

A close-up view of the empennage of the TBM-3E reveals details of the trailing edges of the vertical fin and the horizontal stabilizers, which have lightening holes in them. Visible on the left elevator is the actuator for the trim tab.

Elements of the left side of the fuselage of "Ida Red" are displayed. From evidence gleaned from archival photos, the small vent above the number "7" was for a crew heater that was installed in some TBM-3s and TBM-3Es. A clear view is available of the former stinger machine gun position, which now lacked the triangular side windows and had a window in the rear.

The canopy, turret, and adjacent parts of the fuselage of "Ida Red" are in view. The arch-shaped opening in the rear of the pilot's rollover structure, which contained an instrument panel in the TBF/TBM-1, subsequently contained an APN-1 radio altimeter; this equipment has been removed from this TBM-3E.

The forward parts of the wing-fold joints on the left side of a TBM-3E are portrayed close-up. The yellow mechanism on the side of the center wing section is the wing-locking cylinder. The red object above that cylinder, protruding through the wing, was called the wing-lock flag: it gave the pilot visual evidence that the wings were locked before takeoff. Toward the right, in the corner formed between the inner surfaces of the center and outboard wing sections, are the wing-fold hinges and hydraulic cylinders and their piston rods.

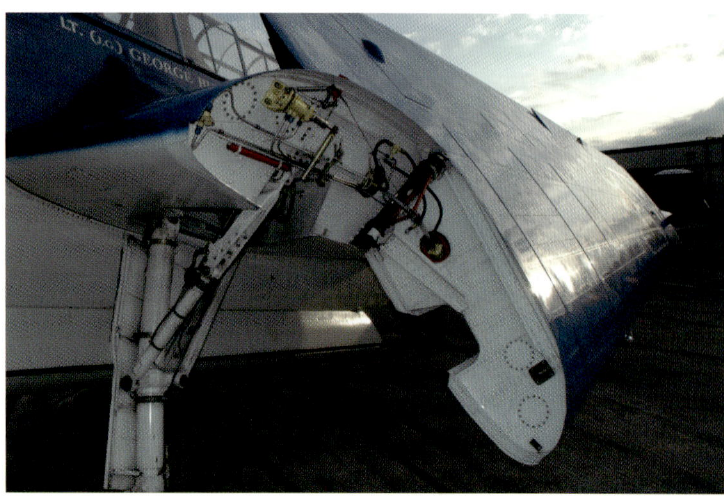

The inner surfaces and locking and operating mechanisms of the left wing are viewed from forward. On the forward part of the inner surface of the outer wing is a small, square object: this is the bracket that captures the locking pin on the wing-locking cylinder when the wing is extended.

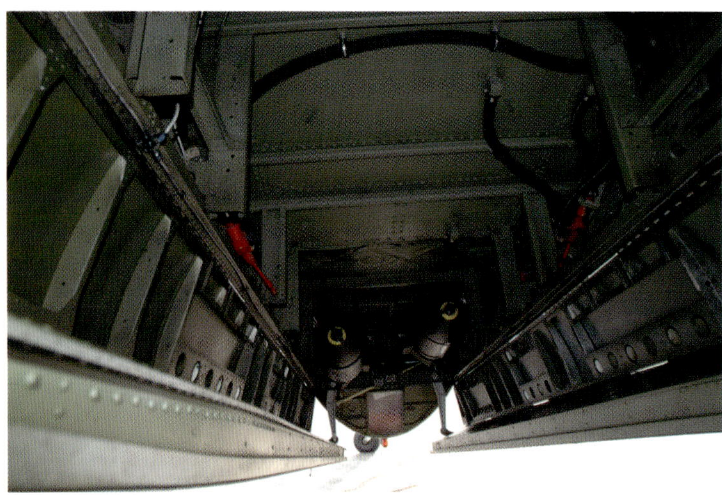

The bomb and torpedo bay of a TBM-3E is viewed from under the forward end, looking aft. Two bombs are mounted on racks in the aft end of the bay; below and aft of them is the bomb-aiming window.

In the forward end of the bomb and torpedo bay of the TBM-3E are the forward operating piston, hydraulic lines, and actuating arms for operating the bay doors. In the bottom of the fuselage to the immediate front of the bay are two 12-volt, 24-amp batteries for delivering supplementary current to the electrical systems of the plane.

Based on converted TBM-3 and TBM-3E airframes, the TBM-3R was introduced during the Korean War as a light transport plane. Its principal role was carrier onboard delivery, or COD: transporting personnel and materials to and from aircraft carriers. The conversion entailed removing the turret, armaments, armor, and other extraneous equipment and installing a new canopy, of which several models were used. This example, flying off the coast of Korea in 1953, is TBM-3R, BuNo 85906, which was assigned to Transport Squadron 23 (VR-23); it appears to have had the original canopy as far back as the former location of the turret, which had a new, clear enclosure. *National Museum of Naval Aviation*

The TBM-3S was a conversion of the TBM-3E airframe to an antisubmarine (ASW) aircraft. This model often operated in conjunction with the TBM-3W radar aircraft as a hunter-killer ASW team. The conversion to the TBM-3S was accomplished by removing the turret and installing a new aft canopy to house a radar operator / navigator's compartment. The aircraft also was fitted with sonobuoy launchers, rocket launchers, and provisions for a searchlight under the left wing. Depth bombs and acoustic torpedoes were transported in the bomb and torpedo bay. An AN/APS-4 radar pod was under the right wing. This TBM-3S was photographed off Key West, Florida, on February 1, 1949. *National Archives*

The Royal Canadian Navy operated TBM-3Ss in the 1950s, one of which is seen here flying above HMCS *Magnificent* around 1953. This plane was assigned to carrier-based Heavier-than-air Search Air Squadron 881 (VS-881). *National Museum of Naval Aviation*

A mixed group of TBM-3Es (first three planes) and TBM-3Ss fly in formation near San Diego, California, on November 24, 1950. In addition to the aforementioned equipment that was installed in the TBM-3S, this aircraft also was provided with an early data-link system, for instantaneously exchanging information electronically with an accompanying TBM-3W2. *National Museum of Naval Aviation*

The TBM-3W, nicknamed the Guppy, was the first airborne early-warning plane. Based on the TBM-3 airframe, it was developed under a program code-named "Cadillac" and featured an AN/APS-20 radar in a huge radome under the belly. As conceived, the main purpose of the TBM-3W was to detect Japanese kamikaze planes long before they arrived over a concentration of US ships. The war ended before the TBM-3W saw operational use, but a follow-up plane, the TBM-3W2, which looked similar to the TBM-3W but had more-sophisticated radar and electronics suitable for antisubmarine warfare, entered active service with US and allied forces during the Cold War. A large radome was mounted on the belly, and vertical fins were added to the horizontal stabilizers to improve directional stability. An example from VS-26 is shown here operating with a TBM-3S in 1951. *National Museum of Naval Aviation*

TBM-3W2, BuNo 91652, from VS-23 is parked on a tarmac at Naval Air Station Oakland, California, on March 28, 1954. Note the several antennas on the bottom of the fuselage aft of the radome. *National Museum of Naval Aviation*

Airdales are tending to a TBM-3W2 from Composite Squadron 21 (VC-21) aboard an antisubmarine-warfare carrier, USS *Badoeng Strait* (CVE-116), around 1948. The TBM-3W2s were converted from TBM-3E airframes. *National Museum of Naval Aviation*

CHAPTER 4

Combat

The first combat experience of the Avenger was inauspicious, with six of the new torpedo bombers being dispatched although assigned to USS *Hornet* (CV-8), to a land base on Midway Island on June 1, 1942. Three days later, the aircraft launched a strike on the Japanese fleet, and only one of the Avengers, Bureau Number (BuNo) 03805, returned to the island, its gunner killed and radio operator wounded. Although pilot Ens. Albert Earnest managed to coax his Avenger, riddled with over seventy bullet holes, back to Midway, it was damaged beyond repair. The hydraulic system had been shot out, the bomb bay doors hung open, and the tailwheel was extended, blocking the field of fire of the ventral gun. Worse, the main controls had been shot away, allowing Earnest to control the aircraft only via the trim tabs. As bad as the initial combat flight of the Avenger was, it was no worse than that of the TBDs it was to replace. Virtually all the venerable Devastators had been lost from *Enterprise*, *Saratoga*, *Hornet*, and *Lexington*. The torpedo squadrons, when reformed, would be equipped with Avengers.

Soon enough, the reequipped squadrons were again launching attacks against the enemy, with the first carrier-launched attack of the Avengers being flown against the Japanese carrier *Ryujo*. While none of the four 500-pound bombs dropped in the first wave found their mark, subsequent coordinated torpedo attacks by Avengers, joined by dive-bombing SBDs sent the Japanese carrier to the bottom.

In the Atlantic, Avengers operating from the escort carrier USS *Bogue* (CVE-9) began attacking enemy U-boats in May 1943 and on the twenty-second of that month succeeded in forcing U-569 to the surface with depth charges. The crew scuttled the boat, and twenty-five of the forty-six crew were rescued by the Canadian destroyer *St. Laurent*, summoned to the scene by the Avenger pilots.

Elsewhere in the Atlantic, the Fleet Air Arm was equipping fourteen squadrons with the big torpedo bomber, supplied under Lend-Lease. In Royal Navy service, the aircraft, which were designated TBF-1B, were first named Tarpon. But in January 1944, the name was changed to Avenger in conformance with US practice. Regardless of name, the Avengers had been modified by Blackburn Aircraft to British standards. Radios, oxygen equipment, and gunsights all were replaced with comparable British equipment. In order to fit in the hangar deck of British carriers, the antenna was fitted with a hinge.

The first Royal Navy squadron to use the TBF was 832 Squadron, which took fifteen Avengers aboard the HMS *Victorious* in January 1943. Those aircraft were actually standard US Navy TBF-1s, rather then British Tarpon Is, and were embarked at Naval Air Station (NAS) Norfolk, Virginia. Actual Tarpon Is entered service in April 1943, when 845 Squadron took delivery of their aircraft at NAS Quonset Point, Rhode Island. As with the US Navy and Marines, the Fleet Air Arm utilized the Avenger not only in an antisubmarine role, but also as a bombing aircraft, striking naval as well as land targets. The most famous of these were raids on the German battleship *Tirpitz*.

In the Pacific, Avengers were involved in some of the US Navy's most decisive victories, with the aircraft being involved in the sinking of twelve Japanese aircraft carriers, six battleships, nineteen cruisers, and twenty-five destroyers and other smaller warships. During the war, US Navy and Marine Avengers dropped 32,700 tons of bombs and shot down ninety-eight enemy aircraft during 46,000+ combat sorties, while suffering 729 losses.

Despite these successes, the Avenger would be the last production torpedo bomber ordered by the US Navy. Almost as soon as the Japanese signed surrender documents, the US began phasing the Avenger out of service. An exception to this were the specialized Avengers such as the TBM-3W. However, by October 1954 the Avenger was solely used for utility and noncombat roles.

In addition to the Royal Navy and Royal New Zealand Air Force, which used the Avenger during World War II, post–World War II many other friendly nations were supplied the aircraft through the Mutual Defense Assistance Program (MDAP). Among these nations were Canada, Uruguay, France, the Netherlands, and, ironically, Japan.

Five Grumman TBF-1s from Auxiliary Scouting Squadron 29 (VGS-29) are in formation during a flight from Naval Air Station Norfolk, Virginia, in September 1942. In October 1942, these planes departed with the squadron on USS *Santee* (CVE-19) to participate in Operation Torch: the invasion of French Morocco. *National Museum of Naval Aviation*

A tractor is towing an Avenger, BuNo 01744 and plane number 13 (on the tail), on the flight deck of USS *Enterprise* (CV-6) in mid-December 1942. During this period the carrier, having recently fought hard in the Naval Battle of Guadalcanal, was conducting training exercises from a base in Espiritu Santo, New Hebrides. This plane had been assigned to VT-10 in the Guadalcanal Campaign and was serving with VT-6 on *Enterprise* when it ran out of fuel and ditched off Espiritu Santo either on November 15 or 16, 1944.

As signified by his brown jersey and helmet, an airdale from the plane captain's crew is securing a rope stay on a TBF/TBM-1 on an aircraft carrier in January 1943. The plane is painted in two-color camouflage of Nonspecular (NS) Blue Gray over NS Light Gray, with Blue Gray on the wing-fold joints and Light Gray on the landing gear. *National Archives*

In a photo likely taken on the same date, and on the same unidentified carrier as the preceding image, aviation fuel handlers clad in red helmets and jerseys are refueling a TBF/TBM-1 numbered 7 on the cowling and the leading edge of the center wing section. A letter "R" followed by one or more partially visible letters or numbers is stenciled in yellow on the folded wing. *National Archives*

The Cactus Air Force—as the motley group of Army, Navy, and Marine aircraft that operated from Henderson Field and other airstrips on Guadalcanal from August 1942 to April 1943 was called—included a number of TBF/TBM Avengers. It is not clear if this TBF/TBM-1 warming its engine at an airfield on Guadalcanal in February 1943 was a bona fide member of the Cactus Air Force or was simply operating temporarily from a land base. *National Archives*

Three crewmen, including pilot Frank Ellsworth of TBF-1, BuNo 47474 and aircraft number 55, assigned to VT-16, are clinging to their plane and awaiting rescue after going overboard during takeoff from USS *Lexington* (CV-16) in the Gulf of Paria, Trinidad, on May 25, 1943. *National Archives*

Airdales, as the crewmen who operated the flight deck were nicknamed, are removing the chocks from the wheels of a TBF/TBM-1 on the flight deck of the Essex-class aircraft carrier USS Yorktown (CV-10) in June 1943. This was likely during the ship's shakedown cruise in the Caribbean during that month. *National Archives*

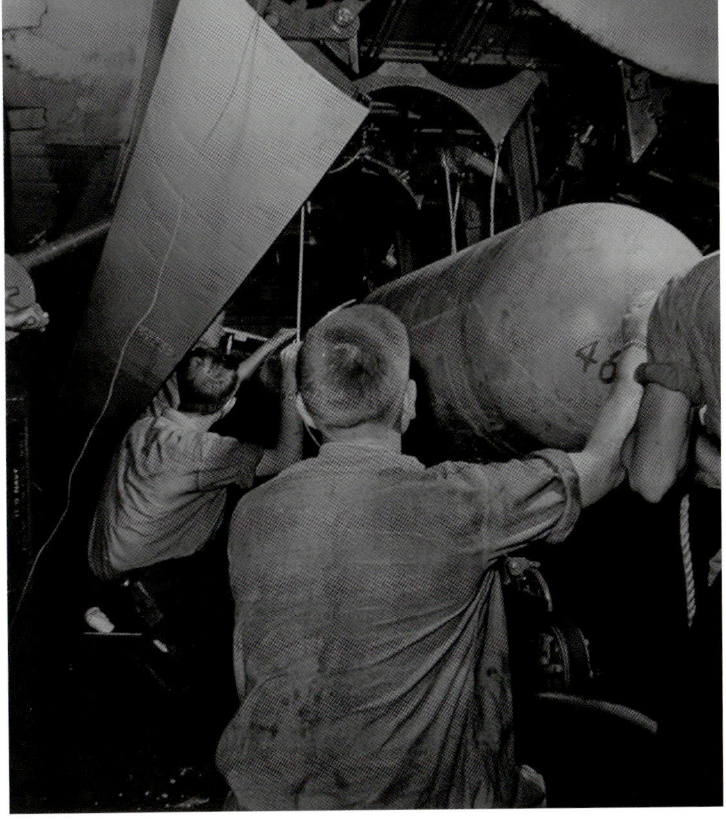

Ordnancemen are hoisting a torpedo into the bomb and torpedo bay of an Avenger on USS *Yorktown* in October 1943. Partially visible to the left, to the side of the right bay door, is a handheld bomb hoist that operated the cables and slings for lifting bombs and torpedoes to the bay. *National Archives*

A weatherbeaten Marine Corps TBF/TBM-1, side number 27-4, with the nickname "Daisy Mae" painted on the cowling, flies over cloud cover near Munda Airfield in the Solomon Islands on July 19, 1943. Eight bombs representing combat missions are painted below the windscreen. *USMC*

A group of Tarpon Mk. Is of the Fleet Air Arm are being prepared for a training exercise at Royal Naval Air Station Hatston, in the Orkney Islands, in the latter part of October 1943. The first two Tarpons are marked "4H" and "4B" on the cowling rings and the ribs of the outer wing sections. *Imperial War Museum*

In another photo taken at Royal Naval Air Station Hatston in late October 1943, Sub-lieutenant W. L. Hughes is boarding the cockpit of Tarpon Mk. I, coded 4Q. All the Tarpons photographed at Hatston on this occasion featured the dramatic downward dips of the darker camouflage color between the leading edge of the wing and the rear of the cowling. *Imperial War Museum*

The pilots of several TBF/TBM-1Cs are awaiting their turns to take off from the light aircraft carrier USS *Monterey* (CVL-26) on December 10, 1943. They, along with the Grumman F6F Hellcat fighters in the background, were about to depart on a combat mission during the Marshall and Gilbert Islands Campaign. The Avengers are painted in three-color camouflage. Note the "0" painted in white on the bottom of the cowling ring of the first plane. *National Archives*

It is Christmas Day 1943, and this Avenger from Air Group 6 has had season's greetings scrawled on the fuselage. The photo was taken aboard USS *Enterprise* (CV-6). Details of the tail landing gear and the tunnel machine gun position are in view. *National Archives*

In an impressive display of US Navy carrier planes warming up for a mission, to the rear of the Hellcats in the foreground are several rows of TBF/TBM-1 Avengers, identifiable by the troughs on the right sides of their cowling tops. The photo was taken on USS *Yorktown* (CV-10) during the Marshall and Gilbert Islands raids in late 1943. *Naval History and Heritage Command*

Wings folded, an Avenger assigned to VT-16 that has just landed is taxiing forward on the flight deck of USS *Lexington* (CV-16) as an F6F Hellcat comes in for a landing in the background. Note how the white paint on the bottom of the fuselage, part of the three-color camouflage scheme, does not reach all the way forward to the cowling ring. *National Archives*

An Avenger in tricolor camouflage, identified on the original label of the photo as a TBF-1, has just caught a wire with its arrestor hook during a landing on USS *Enterprise* during January 1944. A Yagi radar antenna is present under the right wing, and a gun camera is mounted to the front of the windscreen. *National Archives*

During a raid on the massive Japanese base at Truk, in the Caroline Islands, on February 16, 1944, this Avenger, piloted by Lt. (j.g.) R. R. Jones, was hit in the left wing by 20 mm cannon shells from an enemy plane. The wing was in flames as Jones came in for a landing, but he was able to extinguish the fire by landing the Avenger without using flaps. Here, airdales are looking at the damage after the plane safely returned to USS *Enterprise. National Archives*

Two depth bombs are mounted in the rear part of the bomb bay of an Avenger aboard the escort carrier USS *Manila Bay* (CVE-61) on February 24, 1944. To the front of these bombs is a "Fido" Mine-Torpedo Mk. 24, an early, passive-acoustic antisubmarine homing torpedo that entered service in 1943. *Naval History and Heritage Command*

In a dramatic photograph taken in early 1944, a TBF/TBM-1 flies low over a US aircraft carrier in order to drop a written message on the deck during a period of radio silence. Avengers and Grumman Wildcats are spotted on the flight deck; the Avengers are painted in an Atlantic two-color camouflage of Dark Gull Gray and Insignia White. The propeller hubs and the inner parts of the propeller blades are painted what appears to be dull white. *Naval History and Heritage Command*

As seen from the island of the escort carrier USS *Charger* (CVE-30) on April 22, 1944, an Avenger painted in gray and white antisubmarine camouflage is approaching for a landing during a training exercise in Chesapeake Bay. *National Archives*

During preparations for an airstrike on Surabaya, Java, crewmen of the British carrier HMS *Illustrious* are loading bombs in an Avenger Mk. I, since the Tarpon Mk. I had been redesignated recently, during operations in the Indian Ocean in mid-May 1944. The plane's code, 4G, is present on the outer wing rib and the aft fuselage, while the letter "G" is painted on the bottom and the side of the cowling ring. *Imperial War Museum*

Aircrews, officers, and airdales are mixing among Avengers spotted on the forward part of the flight deck of an unidentified aircraft carrier in June 1944. Two-digit numbers are painted in white on the fuselages and vertical fins of the Avengers. Farther forward are several Douglas SBD Dauntless dive bombers, F6F Hellcats, and additional Avengers. *National Museum of Naval Aviation*

Eastern Aircraft TBM-1C, BuNo 46203, with Lt. (j.g.) Anthony M. Peyou at the pilot's controls, has careened off the flight deck and is plowing through the port catwalk during a landing gone wrong on USS *Marcus Island* (CVE-77) on August 8, 1944. Peyou survived the crash, and the war. *National Museum of Naval Aviation*

Loaded with three 5-inch high-velocity aircraft rockets (HVARs) under each wing, the number "6" TBM-3 serving with Composite Squadron 84 (VC-84) comes in for a nose-high landing on USS *Makin Island* (CVE-93) on January 10, 1945. Yagi radar antennas are casting shadows on the undersides of the wings. *Naval History and Heritage Command*

During operations in support of US landings on Luzon in the Philippines on January 12, 1945, the engines of three TBM-3 Avengers are being warmed up and the chocks removed from the wheels while the TBM-3 to the right is being fueled on the carrier USS *Makin Island* (CVE-93). Plane numbers are marked in white on the sides of the cowling rings; to the left is number "1," while the next two Avengers in the foreground are marked, respectively, J3 and J5, with the numbers "3" and "5" on the bottoms of the cowling rings. *National Archives*

This crash of a TBM-1 on an unidentified aircraft carrier on January 23, 1945, was occasioned by pilot error: he néglected to cut the engine in time prior to engaging the arrestor cable. The plane went over the flight deck and damaged a 5-inch gun mount. Pilot and crew were not injured. As a result of the crash, the fuselage was bent at an angle in line with the rear of the wings. *Naval History and Heritage Command*

An Avenger from VT-82 is preparing to move forward into launching position on USS *Bennington* (CV-20) on a rainy, squally day in the Pacific in February 1945. The planes are painted in Glossy Sea Blue and feature the white arrow on the tail and the right wing that was the identification symbol of *Bennington*'s air group at that time. *Naval History and Heritage Command*

This TBM-3, number 113, piloted by Lt. Bob King of VT-82 aboard USS *Bennington*, was proof of the tremendous punishment the Avenger could endure and continue flying. The plane collided with another Avenger during a raid on Chichi Jima, Japan, on February 18, 1945, resulting in the loss of part of the left wing of King's plane. After his crew bailed out, Lt. King managed to fly the Avenger back to his task force, where he made an emergency water landing and was rescued. *Leo Polaski collection*

In the Pacific off San Diego, California, a TBF/TBM-1C, number V34, is about to launch from an unidentified aircraft carrier on a training mission in March 1945. The arm and hand of a crewman may be seen reaching up into the aft cockpit, where radio and electronic equipment was housed. *National Archives*

After World War II, the Avengers that continued to serve in the Navy and Marines were increasingly of the antisubmarine and utility types. Some Avengers were employed in weapons tests, such as this example carrying under its belly an ASM-N-2 Bat radar-guided glide bomb. *Naval History and Heritage Command*

During February 1947, an Eastern Aircraft TBM-3W2 is ready for a catapult launching from the carrier USS *Franklin D. Roosevelt* (CVB-42). The fiberglass radome on the belly of the TBM-3W2 contained the large, rotating radar antenna of the APS-20 search radar. *Leo Polaski collection*

TBM-3E number 514 from Attack Squadron 95 (VA-95) lifts off from the flight deck of USS *Philippine Sea* for a patrol mission in September 1948. Under the left wing, the side number, 514, is preceded by a large letter "D." Note the small vent for a personnel heater on the side of the aft fuselage deck to the rear of the turret. *National Museum of Naval Aviation*

The externally mounted arrestor hook of a TBM-3E has just caught a wire as it prepares to touch down on the flight deck of USS *Philippine Sea* during a cruise in the Mediterranean on August 12, 1948. The plane was serving with Attack Squadron 10A (VA-10A). The side number was 412, and the code "PS" was in big letters on the tail. *National Museum of Naval Aviation*

By early 1950, the Navy was returning some of its older aircraft to active service as part of a naval expansion program. This Avenger at Naval Air Facility Litchfield Park, Arizona, was one example. It has been hooked up to a run-up unit prior to starting the engine. *National Archives*

TBM-3S, BuNo 91166 and side number 411, assigned to VS-21, flies above a submarine running on the surface of the Pacific off the California coast on June 8, 1950. The tail code "BS" was assigned to VS-21 on August 4, 1948. *National Museum of Naval Aviation*

A formation of TBM-3Rs from Air Transport Squadron 21 (VR-21), nicknamed the "Pineapple Airlines," pursue a mission on July 3, 1951. These apparently were among the six Avengers assigned to the Haneda, Japan, detachment of VR-2 in April 1951. *National Museum of Naval Aviation*

Chief Aviation Machinist's Mate George Howell (*left*) and Airman James Moss are hefting a container containing high-priority cargo into the bomb and torpedo bay of a US Navy Avenger somewhere in the Far East on August 18, 1953. *Naval History and Heritage Command*

The engine of a TBM-3R from VR-23 is being serviced at an airfield in Korea on August 29, 1953. An emblem, likely the squadron insignia, is on the fuselage below the windscreen. Some TBM-3Rs, including this example, had a fairing for an antenna on top of the aft part of the canopy. *National Museum of Naval Aviation*

Royal Canadian Navy TBM-3Ss are secured to the flight deck of HMCS *Magnificent* (CVL 21) as the carrier navigates in heavy swells in the North Atlantic in autumn 1953, while participating in Operation Mariner. *National Museum of Naval Aviation*

Passengers are boarding a TBM-3R from the First Marine Air Wing for a flight to a remote Korean airfield on December 5, 1953. The photo gives a good concept of the provisions for entering and exiting the TBM-3R. The personnel shuttle service named the First Marine Air Wing, which operated between hard-to-access airfields, was nicknamed the "Trans-Korean Airlines," and the wing employed nine different models of aircraft in this service. *Naval History and Heritage Command*

Bureau Numbers Assigned through Avenger Contracts

Bureau Number	Make/Model
2539–2540	Grumman XTBF-1
00373–00392	Grumman TBF-1
00393	Grumman XTBF-2
00394–00658	Grumman TBF-1
01731–01770	Grumman TBF-1
05877–06491	Grumman TBF-1
16792–17091	General Motors TBM-1C
22857–23656	General Motors TBM-3
23857–24140	Grumman TBF-1
24141	Grumman XTBF-3
24142–24241	Grumman TBF-1
24242–24340	Grumman TBF-1C
24341	Grumman XTBF-3
24342–24520	Grumman TBF-1C
24521–25070	General Motors TBM-1
25071–25720	General Motors TBM-1C
34102–34105	General Motors TBM-1C
45445–46444	General Motors TBM-1C
47438–47637	Grumman TBF-1
47638–48123	Grumman TBF-1C
53050–53949	General Motors TBM-3
68062–69538	General Motors TBM-3
73117–73498	General Motors TBM-1C
85459–86296	General Motors TBM-3E
91107–92006	General Motors TBM-3E
97532–97672	General Motors TBM-3 – contract canceled before production
97673–97675	General Motors XTBM-4
97676–98601	General Motors TBM-4 – contract canceled before production
102576–104575	General Motors TBM-4 – contract canceled before production
117729–118928	General Motors TBM-4 – contract canceled before production

Painted, in addition to its basic Glossy Sea Blue camouflage, in a colorful, high-visibility scheme of yellow and orange on the wings and empennage signifying its use as a utility plane, a TBM-3E from Experimental Squadron 1 (VX-1) rests on a hardstand at Naval Air Station Boca Chica, Florida, in an undated postwar photograph. *National Museum of Naval Aviation*

A restored Avenger flies above a desert, silhouetted by a low sun. The TBF-1 Avenger arrived at just the right time in the early months of World War II, replacing the obsolete and underperforming Douglas TBD-1 Devastator. The TBF/TBM proved itself in combat a multitude of times in World War II and Korea. *Rich Kolasa*